Clara Joseph's poetry has appeared in the *Toronto Review*, *Mother Earth International*, *Prosopisia: An International Journal of Poetry & Creative Writing*, *Canadian Women's Studies*, the *Journal of Postcolonial Writing*, *Transnational Literature*, the *Journal of Feminist Studies in Religion*, and *Literature and Aesthetics*. Her debut book of poetry, *The Face of the Other* (A Long Poem) (2016), was published by Interactive Publications, Brisbane. The book builds on the ethical philosophy of Emmanuel Levinas and invites the reader to meet the other person.

Joseph is the author of several academic articles and book chapters. Her book, *The Agent in the Margin: Nayantara Sahgal's Gandhian Fiction* (Wilfred Laurier UP, 2008), was nominated by the Writers' Guild of Alberta for the Wilfred Eggleston Award for Non-Fiction Prize. It also won a national Aid to Scholarly Publications Program, Canada. Her edited books include, *Global Fissures: Postcolonial Fusions* (Rodopi, 2006), *Theology and Literature: Rethinking Reader Responsibility* (Palgrave Macmillan 2006), and special issues of the journal *World Literature Written in English – The Postcolonial and Globalisation* (2002) and *Rethinking the Postcolonial and Globalisation* (2002).

Dandelions for Bhabha is a collection of poems that variously respond to theories and theorists popular in literary and cultural studies. In poems ranging from the ridiculous to the meditative, Joseph considers poststructuralist and postcolonial positions on determinism, responsibility, and the general state of affairs of our baffled and baffling world.

She has a PhD in English from York University and is an associate professor of English and an adjunct associate professor of Religious Studies at the University of Calgary.

Interactive Press
The Literature Series

Dandelions for Bhabha

Clara A. B. Joseph

Interactive Press
an imprint of IP (Interactive Publications Pty Ltd)
Treetop Studio • 9 Kuhler Court
Carindale, Queensland, Australia 4152
sales@ipoz.biz
http://ipoz.biz/

First published by IP in 2018
© Clara A. B. Joseph, 2018

All rights reserved. Without limiting the rights under copyright reserved above, no part of this publication may be reproduced, stored in or introduced into a retrieval system, or transmitted, in any form or by any means (electronic, mechanical, photocopying, recording or otherwise), without the prior written permission of the copyright owner and the publisher of this book.

Printed in 11 pt Baskerville.

 A catalogue record for this book is available from the National Library of Australia

Dedicated to Prof. Joy Sebastian Kuttickattu – Joychai – mentor & teacher. You made me love literature.

Acknowledgments

Cover image: *Dreaming Fantasy*, by Andrew Paul (Andy's Abstract's), the abstract artist from Bangalore, India.

Book design: David P Reiter

A Social Sciences and Humanities Research Council (SSHRC) Standard Research Grant (2004-2010) supported research on the literary and cultural theories on which this collection is based.

The words and phrases in single quotes in "The Death of the Author's Mother" are adapted or adopted from Roland Barthes' posthumously published, *Incidents*.

The italicized lines in "The Prophet's Cup" are adapted from Cormac McCarthy's novel, *The Road*.

"Spivak" appeared in a different version in *Canadian Woman Studies*. 31.

"Jus' Thinkin'" appeared in a different version in *Transnational Literature*. 8.2 (May 2016).

"Gandhi's Art" appeared in a different version in *Prosopisia: An International Journal of Poetry & Creative Writing*. Vol. 1 (2008).

"Nothing Outside," "Eternity, Now!" and "To kiss a little book" appeared in *Literature & Aesthetics*. 27.2 (2017).

"Jerome is One." *Mother Earth International: All Women's Issue – Section 1*. 7.1.

I am grateful to David P Reiter, Emily Brain and Michael Kenyon for their valuable editorial suggestions and to Tom Wayman for proposing the title for this collection.

Sunny, Jijo, and Jiji – for unwavering love and support.

Contents

Descartes' Lover	1
Nothing Outside	3
Descartes' Lover	5
Metaphysics for Derrida	7
Gandhi's Art	9
Asked to Write Something Colonial	11
Thesis	12
The Business of Life	13
Law of Nature	15
My Dead Cousin's Secret	17
The Voice in the Desert	19
Brown Ghost in White	21
Telos	22
Giving Directions in Calgary	24
Those Long and Chubby Fingers	25
Constructed Relative	26
Pinging the Pong	27
A Grim Tale	30
There is something about Derrida	32
Jus' Thinkin'	35
Let's Talk	37
The Death of the Author's Mother	39
You Blamed the Hen	41
Remembering Paul Adolph Michel Deman	42
Eternity, Now!	50
Truth and Error in a Kaleidoscope	51
Consequentialism at War	53
Figure Skating	55
Groundbreaking	56
Pining	58

Speaking with the Dead	60
What You Said	61
Dandelions for Bhabha	64
migrants	65
Spivak	66
Jerome is One	68
Jus' Thinkin'	69
Theorizing Difference	71
Singing of Difference	72
from the Canadian pew	75
Prophet-Prostitute	76
Translation	77
To Talisman	**79**
History	81
The Prophet's Cup	83
Only Hands	85
The Person in my Eye	86
Are You a Feminist?	88
The Taj Mahal	90
To Talisman	91
Milk for Ganesha?	93
Compassionate Choice	94
La La Liberté	95
Soodo Klaasik	97
Friends of Thomas More	98
Professional Secrets I	99
To . . .	100
Professional Secrets II	101
To kiss a little book	102
Santa!	103
War and Peace 101: Final Exam	104

Descartes' Lover

Nothing Outside

Il n'y a rien hors du texte.
– Jacques Derrida

There is nothing outside,
Absolutely nothing

Noticeable outside;
Nothing standing, there,

Looking back from the outside;
No one coming, none disappearing;

No sun hidden within
A shadow;

No one bending, not
One sitting,

None moving as if to
Lie;

No rancid corpse
Stretched

Out
To be eaten;

No whiff of wolves prowling, no cursing serpent
Lying,

None there to quickly strike
A heel,

Or steal;
None camouflaged out there,

No one to lay
A hand,

Kill,
Nor one who can redeem;

Nothing whatsoever
There:

Descartes' Lover

Cogito ergo sum.
– Rene Descartes

The lover caresses her own rising
womb, and displays the twitching nerve's
rhythmic pulse to her determining will;
and dreams lap in the dark.
She too is caught
in a hushed presence.

She puts one foot forward, releases
the other of the burden
in an unerring balancing act
of a sailor treading on sea. Exhausted
she becomes salt, forever
beckoning her beloved.

The one who looks is never transformed
into stone; the hero's mirror will be smashed
into smithereens by her love. She is a goddess
sweating a river. She is you
and me, turning transparent
into water. The wave that dashes, sprinkles
a thousand drops, scatters,
dazzles; captures the rainbow shuddering
in each tiny tear that she gathers
into a single tsunami. She is black
Saraswati, pretty with a book and a guitar

   rolling toward him
   with the gentle
   swish of thoughts draped
   over one shoulder, revealing
   the cleavage of her soul;

she is the one who rushes seismic
to him with nerves, with
eyes and hands.

Metaphysics for Derrida

The center is not a fixed locus but a function, a sort of non-locus in which an infinite number of sign-substitutions came into play.
– *Jacques Derrida*

                This space bustling
With men, women, and children
Gathered to hear, they said, a *ghazal*.
A *what?* I asked, then came with them,
Came along to see such performance

(to know what I did not know
knowing not what they knew).

Derrida began with a *salaam*,
Met with deafening applause
From men, women, children,
Continued on a deep note

        Sustained to its dire end,
While I twisted and turned,
My poor legs threatening to go
To sleep, and I myself followed.

I startled awake to Wah! Wah!
And heavy thumping on my back.
I challenged him then and there,
To which my neighbor quoted,
                in a trance:

"The center is not the center!"

Followed with yet another Wah!
Where did the center go? I asked,
Struggling to wake my legs.
The crow stole it, offered his son,

The one who had been watching
Me dream-up their performance.
Sshh! his mother said,

    You know there is no crow.

Wow! I said, Wow! Wow! Wow!

Gandhi's Art

I would reverse the order. I see and find Beauty in Truth or through Truth. . . . Whenever men begin to see Beauty in Truth, then true Art will arise.
— *Mahatma Gandhi*

Sole figure hanging at the Vatican, the vision
        paralyzing, now reviving,
the viewer edging to the back, to
        the sides, edging close, to his meaning.
Such theology of the body, such art
        that dismissed the unknown flesh,
made known the name and
the face.

No artist dead in this art when a viewer
        comes to more life, wetting
at the source of the artist's intent,
the art
        overflowing, the viewer drenched.
None mad in this world of artist and
        viewer, none so doomed to death;
no artist so majestically autonomous,
none
        not subject to the law, if human.

Such art, monstrously, dared the fact
        of history, mowed down the wall of
exclusion
        which called only one the Son
of God
        or stained one with the red of sword.
The *Bible* his art became, non-violent the *Gita*
        as his art, and the artist manifested
as God's son,
        the heart a bloody world, a battlefield
of good and evil within, a troubled messiah.

Art: is, to be, not the artifice nor the devious
    but that thou art, in the being, to
truth's end
    Gandhi's chant scatters to the winds
the pages
of history and gathers in the breath of truth.

Breath alighting on adolescent waters, without
    manners, looks, or a shape to speak of,
gently coaxed to form this world
    and all its wonders;
        one step enough for me.

Here, the wonder that spoke to the Wonder
    culled *out* of the object anonymous,
wonder of wonders, a human breathing
    such breath
in such a Mover, an artist inspired!

Asked to Write Something Colonial

How about my skin?
If against white.
Death of a beloved?
If the whites did it.
How about tears?
If a white caused it.
How about laughter?
If at the white.
Um . . . how about sex?
If with the white.
But you know inter-marriage is not permitted?
That's very colonial.

Thesis

Deconstruction is justice.
– Jacques Derrida

What *should* you write about? What's in vogue? New
Historicism, these days: it is good to quote old Greenblatt
Or else you will not be thought a scholar; unless you are
Looking, of course, at the top of your own navel, another's
Only so long as it is still a navel that is being deliberated –
All navels, having cut asunder chains, should certainly be
                                  Most respected.

But if your teacher is a postcolonialist, your mother-in-law
An imperialist, and your own dear father dead? What then?
What if your boss whose profits you are supposed to share
Is a postmodernist? Wouldn't it be better for your work
To be in postmodernism, then? Yet if there is something out
There – a job advertised perhaps in Children's Literature,
Why should you not make that your sudden specialty even if
Children bore you and *they* will have nothing to do with you?
                                  But. But.

What is it in you that is stirring at the jerk
Of a limb blown up, split wrist to elbow
By institutionalized violence – perfectly legal – represented
In a storybook as so right and normal? They tell you
You are over-reacting? You shouldn't be bothered by every
Sneeze on earth? Yet, yet, something about that limb remains.
Something of the woman? Or the limb that lies apart?
Something keeps you
Awake. And, you think, if you do not write you too might
explode,
Split open, maybe a bit more, mid-line, below your collarbone,
                    Where it all, after all, begins.

The Business of Life

King David reclines,
rather sits,
vibrating eagerness on
a ten-stringed
kinnor. The sweet scent of the *kinnaram*,

the sandalwood from Ind's shores, has glided
inland after Arab waters, to refresh his hands with
a stubbornness so subtle, so soft, so simply nice.

    The plucked string sets forth into the universe alone,
gifting those with ears a dewdrop's tinkle on
an unfurled petal or a leaf
plain and simple.

King David has upon this harp learnt
the art of there-there-thereing the weeping
child, of shoo-shoo-shooing the devious
wolf grown friendly towards the flock, of soothing
Saul's soul otherwise stretched

across envy's spikes. The child,

the wolf, and the king thus share the melodious message. All are
in different ways redeemed. Or so thinks the Kinnor now
swaying gently in love's sturdy arms. But,
what if, and this is the literary truth,

thousands of years have just sped away like
so many minutes in any given day? The strings number
now less than ten. Several lie about, haggard,
over a soundboard gone awry, the body broken in

so many places. The fact is, breath yet remains in
two strings taut to the tip. These make song

this world has yet to hear elsewhere. This world
does not comprehend or count as it might the worth of
David who carefully oils its behind. There is
no more time for a song. So.

The muffled tune sits nervous and tiny: aching initially,
dulling finally, utterly doomed in the dirty smog.
When someone touching it feels
the slight, trashing it is deemed a right. Surely,

there is no crime where a sob is
stifled, where death pangs are felt
out of sight, and pleasure is bought with
The power to push out the petty and all pain whatsoever.

Last strings are loosened, donated to visible charity bent on
building a future for those boisterous and bold who
bang the bedside bongos. No lyre shall be heard now
there are no more lullabies. Stringless, the kinnor is tossed
just the day before the city museum puts out a call for
King David's harp.

The wind that once played on the strings, well,
it brought home at last the business terms:
to soothe Saul's madness in the new millennium
                        the music is worth a million.

Law of Nature

A miracle is a violation of the laws of nature; and as a firm and unalterable experience has established these laws, the proof against a miracle, from the very nature of the fact, is as entire as any argument from experience can possibly be imagined.
– David Hume

Nature to be commanded must be obeyed.
– Francis Bacon

I'd said we'd stay to count
The baskets, return them to owners,
You or I could then thrash them into a line
And out the narrow wicket;
But you would have none of it.

You sent us to bed in a boat.
A quiver of your right eyebrow
Told me you meant business.
So, we left. We watched you
File the exit of thousands
Wanting more, then more,
And more, for no known reason,

Just wanting more, taking all
That they can, and you with them.
Now we're wet and salted like fish
On land that receded in the night
When I might have slept
By the unfamiliar rock, and you

Might pray to heart's content—
'O my God, don't let them catch me!'
Or whatever else it is you pray.
I know, but just can't bother
With this incessant storm
Now striking, over-turning

My little boat
And us as we strain to still

The uproar with this old oar –
Wretched attempts of wood,
Wind, wood, water boiling
Raging, at God knows what!
That! That! That! Go! Go! Away!
What is That?! That passes us!

That returns! Speech through the booming
Storm as terror terrifyingly repeats
It is I it is I it is I it is I it is I it is I It is I it is I it is I it is I it is
You! I sigh. I cannot help smiling and forget
Salt and sting of sea.

I had known you couldn't stay
In the refuge to which you'd fled
With prudent fear of philosophers
And rulers. Some philosopher-kings!

The sinews of my arms pull at the oar
Straining against you, and you
Walk over the water
Like any lover.

My Dead Cousin's Secret

No testimony is sufficient to establish a miracle, unless the testimony be of such a kind, that its falsehood would be more miraculous, than the fact, which it endeavors to establish.
– David Hume

My dead cousin declared his intent to tread water so full
In our pond right beside plantain groves at the back of the house
In full view of busy servants and tattlers, trouble-makers.

I, his faithful and aid, then the rest sworn to allegiance,
Listened in awe as he swore to tread water Sunday night at eight.
Knowing when he thus spoke it was done we too swore
Not to keep it a secret but shout it to all when we could
Yet so casually that adults hearing should gasp, "Who would walk?!"

So, when my aunt's blouse flew off the taut washing line to the pond
I took a deep breath and casually said: "Enron can... Sunday... Oops!"
Well-aimed oops now familiar to aunty she ran after me.

Caught, grip firmer the second I blurted under duress full loud:
"A big secret! Enron! Sunday night sharp at eight will walk pond!"
Answers verified sternly confirmed with five cousins then stopped,
Making aunty full sworn to sharing news so good to the house, and
Servants signaling three worried neighbors, the media they turn
Telling priests, mendicants, who send us red *sindhoor* in plantain leaf
And *ladoos*.

We gathered by the pond auspiciously to eat big *ladoos*
When a wind raised the wrap of *sindhoor*, set it on our full pond,
Beckoning him to walk the waters to retrieve the red'ning,
Wonder now worrying his young brows; we demanded magic
At dusk Friday for the walking-over-the-waters-Sunday-night,
For the wind had lifted the *sindhoor*, laid it on our full pond.

We debated an hour; Enron said he'd walk just this once
On our pond over water and we stared into the Friday darkness
To see him waving high his hands walking the still waters
Returning *sindhoor*-less to us standing at safe distance, scared;
Told me then to take down the taut line that lets him tread
Our full pond, ghost-walk waters at eight each Sunday night.

The Voice in the Desert

The fable of intelligible freedom.... Thereby one achieves the knowledge that the history of moral sensations is the history of an error, the error of responsibility which rests on the error of freedom of the will.
– Friedrich Nietzsche

For what is man without desires, without free will, and without the power of choice but a stop in an organ pipe?
– Fyodor Dostoevsky

The invader moves in, his feet shod for safety,
Feeling not once the tickle of the sands that are his
Today. He tells himself he is lord of all
That he surveys, yet cannot read the signs
Of damnation that mark
A people less than human.

The cruelest century has begun, my people,
Begun by men and then women, finally children
Thinking they have no choice. You see how determined
They are to save you and me: little lips trained to hum
The praises of nations' dead sergeants; mothers forced
To whimper into their children's dirty laundry;
Fathers and sisters made to fight
Over stupid expedient errors
Before they don once more their uniforms
To visit us with the points of bayonets
Announced by the distant rifle shot.

The humming birds have begun
their slow ascending rounds far above
Wondering eyes that stare unblinking and
Alert ears attuned to the whirring buzz until –
The bombs fall, and all hell is loosed upon
Creation's harmony of laughter, insults, and sighs.

They are under orders, my people, under
Those who are also under… so many
Papers carefully drafted, blueprints of
Where exactly to jab
To draw water
With the blood.

Their armies no longer march; they fly
And then scuttle away in machines so that we
Cannot simply reach out to them. But you will.
You will stretch out your arms to them.
Then you, my people, shall sing.
You shall sing you are absolutely
Free to reach out to them even though they continue
To loot in the name of
Being sent.

Brown Ghost in White

You figured forth, silent and brown in white
robe not seen these days of business:
shirt, pants tight to hips. These
loosened in private to the channeled
world.

You sallied forth.
(Eyes that see not,
ears that hear not, touch me not!)
All is caught in, yet, caught in

unbroken rightness,
right, freedom, freedom, freedom.... All expressed in
expression, of expression, on
expression-sharpened wordings –
uncensored.

You bodied forth where elected elite feed
freedom and right freely conceived:
a world of no wrongs or wrongfulness.
All is determined, pre-determined,
constructed, deconstructed. Technologies
remain in poverty-ridden neighborhoods,
in colonial hotels of us and them, other, yet another
voice and my simple question is: when did you break
your silence?

Telos

The end (telos), that for which a thing is done....
– Aristotle

It could be shown that all the names related to fundamentals, to principles, or to the center have always designated an invariable presence—eidos, arche, telos, energeia, ousia *(essence, existence, substance, subject)* aletheia, transcendentality, consciousness, God, man, and so forth.
– Jacques Derrida

What do you think you're going to do
After the end
Of this course
On Voltaire's nose?
It's not curiosity or anything
Like that, mind you (which noses are sometimes
Entitled to), it's just to know where you are
Heading at the end
Of such investigation into a
                                            nose
Made, as Voltaire says, for spectacles,
Not the other way round,
And not in the least for you
To see or for your nose
To smell, but
Where are you heading?

I really am not sure,
Professor, I'd like to go
To a foreign land and teach
Them English or so? Perhaps
Just work here, maybe, you know,
In a bar where I'm used
To serving anyway, and earn
Money to boot, not bad at all;
Really!!!

To tell you the truth, I'm not sure
But might end up here,
Working at the university
Bar, just to stick around poets
Or profs and overhear
Ideas, some not bad at all – booze
Broadens horizons – but who knows,
I might go South to teach English
And a break will do me good before
I, maybe, return
To another degree, maybe teach
Voltaire's nose
To smarter folk!

You speak English rather well and so should
Teach in another land or, as you say,
You've worked in a bar and know your way.
Because Lucretius says: what happens to exist is the cause
Of its use –
Universities are made for bars;
Therefore, you shall serve.

Giving Directions in Calgary

(acknowledging Natasha Trethewey)

You can reach your destination if you leave now, but
there is no turning back for you.

Where you go will be unfamiliar.
There is no going home. So, do this:

get out of the bus loop first and head for the Chinook arch;
exit from university life is a matter of a

minute. Watch out for players on your left tossing a foul ball
from the ghostly site of a bygone Olympics into

the determining road where so many steps away the sky
settles in your path. You know you are bound to touch

the heavens some second of this short trip up the road; turn
at the green light turning amber, then red; turn right; reflect

on the name of the road you are riding on – Unwin.
To confirm the omen, in front of you suddenly rises

a cross at the end of a stricken dome. Take
a left but watch the stubborn symbol at your rear

peeping past so many free-trade stores; the lights, the lights,
the lights again, let you proceed only as far as the sudden right

through the narrow path and the emergency; here the script is washed
white in blood – you have arrived.

Those Long and Chubby Fingers

I cull him from my past
ever so often
and clasp his fingers,
mine in his.
Then kiss those fingers
one by one
knowing all along
that there are none,
that what I'm kissing is worms
on my father's skeleton
or just my own.

Constructed Relative

Constructed worlds worn out with words that worlded,
One world reworded the First, Second, Third, Fourth, of
Nietzscheans who never once foresaw such uneven birth,
Saussurean rebirths in chthonic damp, the slime of words
Trumped up then trashed as befits someone's will to power,
Riches unaccounted in gems, spices, another's land, now oil,
Unchallenged, imitated instead in compliments to the recent past:
Capitalists genuflecting to colonialists, to Adam, Locke, Mill,
Third worlds thrashing about for some place within their First,
European unions worried, fretting how best to reword or
Deconstruct the worded world with the will to power, once more.

Relative worlds these, reviewed, revised, returned to their places,
Empires re-labeled, re-presented in a shirt, suit, tie: Globalized!
Love's labors all lost, interred, where machines, technologies,
Academies, the media and their army, confer in one conspiracy:
Truth is here defined, redefined, again, yet again, as relative truth;
I become a personal pronoun, the space of a subject – dispensable;
Virtues dissolve at the onslaught of postmodern ideologies;
Eternity itself a narrative once told by some universal fool.

Pinging the Pong

There is no mind absolute or free will, but the mind is determined for willing this or that by a cause which is determined in its turn by another cause, and this one again by another, and so on to infinity.
— Baruch Spinoza

The concept of narcissism — that is to say, the discovery that the ego itself is cathected with libido, that the ego, indeed, is the libido's original home, and remains to some extent its headquarters.
— Sigmund Freud

Man can will nothing unless he has first understood that he must count on no one but himself; that he is alone, abandoned on earth in the midst of his infinite responsibilities, without help, with no other aim than the one he sets himself, with no other destiny than the one he forges for himself on this earth.
— Jean-Paul Sartre

The player well-practiced is all mind
and eyes. She bursts with oxygen,
to which she surrenders her being.

She acts

to the tune of her learning and is relaxed
in her dreaming where her wishful blues in
pinks
tint yellow into
gold,
greens and lavender,
sink into the lark's melody to which she sways
to the beat of her chase:
                      tap, tap, tap
transforms, startles even her with boom,

the boom of a drumming. She is not alone yet knows

she is the one dealing a click that crashes
the plastic past the net in the sudden
swoop of a hawk.
      The mind shooting

the expanse wonders at a celestial
gift – freedom of will:
        will, aim, hit,
move, place, turn, pick, begin at the end,
breathe the win. Entrapped,

she is not a player.

She is you and me, very busy with things
she must learn to surrender, teaching herself
to train all over. She is at ease as she poses

again, for the service and a smash.
She is the postmodern star refusing to be
driven by her libido
        or someone's ideology
as she draws the ball into a
    C
     h
      i
       n
      o
      o
     k
     over

the green table and becomes the rhythm
of her own sacred game: her limbs take over

the bounce of the hollow ball, the paddle
subtly encircles her form,
                              as she turns into
wind that sweeps across the plain. In this
contact of a little bat, ball, and being she knows

she is moving the rocky mountain to
the destination of her choice.

A Grim Tale

It's been many years since I began to keep my eyes on
The retreating forest line. The concrete has only grown,
One invisible step at a time, always forward, karate-like,
Farther and farther into the hallowed grove. I watch for you
Who left a soldier's side when suddenly the sun

Sank into the trees. You left this place gifting the man
Two precious things: what he mustn't and what he must.

He must neither refuse nor
Drink the cup offered nocturnally.
He must pretend to
Be sound asleep. To be invisible
He must wear the little cloak.

These he hastily took, turned earnest, success-oriented.
These he hastily took from you, before he told
The King that he was a suitor, before he turned
King himself in a snatch, at your expense. I watch
For you, hoping you will one day step out of the brief green,
Your hair white as pollinating daffodils, your limbs
Never told from autumn twigs, to claim
Your rightful place in this barren land. Be our queen.

There is nothing written about you to tell me
You have rights. Just responsibilities undertaken
Naturally that point to one radical thought: you and
Yours are people. I watch for you, 'cause twelve princesses –
Women really – wait behind closed doors with worn-out souls,
Having not danced. They simply cannot sleep;
They possess no little cloak and yet are invisible like you.
These children too sinned – never challenged a father's right
To kill suitors who slept. None told the King all daughters were
Really people. You must have heard – the old King is dead.

The soldier now rules. Much is done for the sake of peace.
Enemies are daily killed, and the tale is briefly told:

Once upon a time a soldier met
An old woman who asked him
Where he was going.

Perhaps you do not wish to leave the haunt of beasts
That never cage each other or kill their own. Perhaps
You know it is not so here. Yet, perhaps, you shall return.
And this has been my hope; this is my most desperate hope:
What drove you that day to the edge of the dying forest
Shall drive you here again. I just wanted you to know
Tomorrow is my turn and we are all unseen, all victims, all
peace. So,
When you come bring a bagful of good advice to close our
Restless eyes, but, most of all, this time don't forget
To gift the little cloak that will make us all visible at last.

There is something about Derrida

There is something about Derrida that makes me anxious,
    The bump on my head like a swollen gooseberry still,
There is something about Derrida that makes me say
        Beware of old men, my friend, beware!

        There *is* something about Derrida
        There is *something* about Derrida
        There is something *about* Derrida

    That makes me want to take a step back.

When I (with the gooseberry) married Renu
And a little head appeared between her legs one day,
I went ahead, named her Maya
                to spite her old man.
But when I held the little bottom in my palm
And wondered at
    lids,
        nose,
            lips and chin,
ears,
        I knew – this was Maya!

            Whose tiny bottom I held in my palm.

So, when I see, hear, or smell Derrida,
I'm anxious about his bottom, his big-fat-bottom where

    Things
        fall

        apart

And not because the center cannot hold

As I hold my Maya's
                              bottom,
Now grateful to the old man for proving my philosophy
Against the temple's stone pillar,

My brains colliding with the not-nothing of the philosopher's stone
                    (Stone! Can you believe it?! Stone!)
He refuses to postulate as philosophers ought;
Rams my head, instead, against the pillar-stone,
          A coconut bump that I receive shriveling, at last, into this
gooseberry,

For having expounded, with premises and conclusions intact,
That all was, indeed, illusion—
Maya!
"Then, this too," he replies,
breaking an hour's patient listening and my head
(I was philosophizing),
"Is *Maya*!"

                    There is something about Derrida, something,
                    something,

That makes me nervous,
That makes me want to warn *him* of glum old men
          Who might gift his bottom with a resounding present,
A thrashing that would send him howling;

          A stinging presence across his bottom
          Constructing him and his meaning
(Let him finger his own bottom),
Two blooming buns, bereft of their center; and he
                    Calling on the Center, for once.

Jus' Thinkin'

Let's Talk

We need to talk.
Come here, will you?
We need to talk.

What caused those sighs?
Those broken sleeps?
Those fits of rage and love?

I want to know what really passed
Your eyes
Behind the newspaper

Around which I passed
Cups and cups of tea.

I thought I knew you.
Now I want to hold you.
To know you. Really.

To share those burdens
That rose in your heart
And I barely heard
Or thought were physical.

So, I brought you freshly squeezed lime juice
With a little sugar, sometimes salt, added.
But I heard them again – those deep sighs.

And I switched on the fan to comfort you
In all that sweltering heat, around us.

That you could not be comforted
Now I know
As the sighs have begun in me, your child.

And when neither coke nor snow can stop these sighs
I long, long, to know you.

What was your past,
My father?
What were those burdens?
Those sins
That made you look far away;
That sent up one sigh after another?

Speak!
Before it's too late.
I'm busy here in Canada.

Speak to me from the leisure of your grave.

The Death of the Author's Mother

By a radical reversal, instead of putting his life into his novel, as is so often maintained, he made of his very life a work for which his own book was the model. . . .
– Roland Barthes

No misreadings here, Monsieur, just a reader's ways
At work when works have burned
To texts, authors read
Dead. And you have zipped to work, to teach
Morocco
Your French tongue, the language, your semiotics
Surprising you and your protectorate: *cul/con/queue*.
So much so that all unzip
In colonial obedience.
To you, Happiness at Mehiula: 'the whole ballet of little
Visits, the warmth, the djellaba, and reading
Lacan!'

I read: not you, M., just language that
Performs
The French tongue,
The hand of Mohammed, another
Mohammed, yet another Mohammed,
Woven into text
In an eternal present whose past has buried
The dead
Author.
A Mohammed again, 'this hand too
Slow for his thought or passion… the hand cut
Off from any voice…' the carefully groomed
Hand
Washed, after the shoeshine boy has bent
Over your feet.

The one you gift an Eiffel Tower, a phallic souvenir,
The other will gift you tomatoes
From a store,
A third pays *you* his bus fare for a ride
You offer.
Your gaze daring, unsettling, you say,
You are interested.
A semanticist electrified! 'A silent dawning of meaning
Observed in someone's eyes.' Monsieur, you have
Learnt then of meaning that you, yes, M., brought about when
Not dead but alive
With imprudence.

Such subjects, Monsieur, become
Objects. Henrietta, your dear mother, captured, was five then.
You notice her gesture, 'awkward,' one finger in a hand
As children often do,
Before they become mothers,
Their past real as the present, for once, Monsieur, and you
Find your mother again in this photo:
Child of the past, your loved subject. But,
Monsieur, he too was
'Not more than five,' when you – in bed, like dead –
Saw him in shorts, knock on a door,
'Adjust his crotch.'

You Blamed the Hen

(for child songwriter, Mareena Chandy)

for pecking at your
eight-year-old song-writing:

the sun and
the beautifullest Fall along
with the pure snow,
pendragon sister, darling
mother, to my father
on Father's Day,
Just tell the truth,
God the One (not yet done, you say) – like grain
all over the vacationing
verandah

and now, vacations later,

sixteen whole years of wisdom knows
the place to find pages
of feeling precious is tucked

inside a grown-up chick.

Remembering Paul Adolph Michel Deman

Old Ousep, born and bred by the old
Kochi synagogue, closed
his lids.

He waited for the end –
his burial in a foreign land
his grandchildren called:
home. But,
he himself,
his ancestors
had for two thousand years or more called
God's own country[1]
native land. Lids shut tight,

taut with impatience, he awaited
the end of things – one hundred and one goodbyes.
but hardly had the first layer of mud fallen,

the thud on his roof not unlike
the monsoon hails
hitting verandahs,
sending the pirates back,

than he heard someone next door speaking:
the gibberish in his left ear was English.
that much he realized, and even learnt, upon his death, to reply.

Names almost exchanged,
the weather commented on,

> de Man,
> that was his name,
> confirmed he wasn't
> Pamela Mordecai's.

---
[1] Kerala, in India, is advertised by the tourism sector as "God's own country."

> She had big trouble with
> 'the' and called the Son
> of Man "De Man."

I hear you, said Ousep, unable to stem the blast,
but who is
"De Man"?

> I am, he said, and that is my point: this "I" is
> a pronoun, a personal pronoun, this "I" on which I wrote, I,
> this I on which I wrote two whole books in my lifetime....

Two books! Ousep exclaimed,
unable to extend a hand in congrats,
repeated, two whole books! And shook his head,
a weeny bit.

> De Man understood or was grateful: this "I"
> and I'll say it again, the "I" is but
> a personal pronoun.

That too I've learnt now, returned Ousep eagerly,
grateful for quick grammar lessons,
of an I and a personal pronoun
six feet deep and not so bad
in this sudden mud.

I, said Ousep, I is a personal pronoun, and imagined the other nod;
so, asked again, but who is De Man?

> I am, the voice
> returned, not Mordecai's, of course, oh no! My name, he
> said, is
> de Man and yours Ousep, I understand – I being a
> personal pronoun.
> and you too Christian?

No, a Jew, returned Ousep,
when silence lingered
beyond politeness forcing him to say,
Yahudan, this time, and then, Jew,
again, then again, are you a writer? How long have you been
writing?

Silence in such a personal pronoun Ousep found now
a bit troubling.
How are you? Will the mud hold? Good to meet you.
Then heard sighing low monotones of how long,

> How very long, he had been writing;
> writing while so young and all; writing
> into old age too; what is there but
> writing,
> playing,
> languaging.
> Lessons in linguistics

Cut short by old curiosity: what did you write
about?

> Non-question, came the response.

Non-question, Ousep learnt. So much
to learn in this fresh soil,
this new land.

> You mean what I wrote about, what I wrote meant, what
> is the meaning of what
> I wrote, you mean, but there is no meaning that is final,
> there is
> no final meaning, no meaning…

Ousep caught on quickly: and that
is your meaning! Believed

the personal pronoun nodded at
quick comprehension.

> I am, after all, a good teacher, producing
> the *Gayaaaaaaaaatri Spivak* and many
> more, many, many, more…

Now me?
Ousep queried hopeful doubtful.
The stillness felt
unfriendly.
He'd perhaps been buried at the border of another
cemetery where lay personal pronouns
in close proximity.
Then heard new sighing

> Low monotones of how long, of how long,
> how very long,
> he had been writing; writing while so young and all; writing
> into old age too; what is there but writing.
> playing
> languaging,
> Said the personal pronoun proffering one more lesson,
> the same, in linguistics,

Cut short by old curiosity: what did you write about?

> Non-question that, the voice returned,
> classic instance of seduction you are, for you
> form and meaning,
> knowing and dreaming, viewing,
> are all the same in dangerous liaison of this
> aesthetic ideology, for you this lesson—
> from Literature where like the sun hidden
> in a shadow lies truth in error,
> fact in fiction
> and fiction in fact prompt Literature writing's archetype –

> the honesty of an allegory's transparency
> where its truth of artifice suffices,
> where it simultaneously asserts, denies,
> authority, for you this lesson – of redemption, Oh, Ousep!

I'm lost,
confessed Ousep, where I come from
we have tales written, tales told,
none too dangerous,
though writers and tellers are
and often jailed. Just then some glimmer of
understanding dawning
in this darkness six feet deep, Ousep continued:
but if you are a personal
pronoun and your work such fruit,
grammar, linguistics, then this mix of work....

> Text! said the personal pronoun,
> don't you understand *now*?
> At least when you are down and under?!

Sorry, said Ousep, Text, said Ousep,
Least bewildered, for textbooks plenty
he had wrapped, labeled, for children
all grown so big,
so big to fly away
to this foreign land *now*.
He dug for sorrow, nostalgia perhaps.
Found none; returned to the glimmer that dawned
a moment ago. Ah! Yes! If you are a personal
pronoun and your text tapioca of grammar, linguistics, then this
mixing

of text and meaning needs treating, even jailing perhaps.
How on earth can a personal pronoun be
held but under this earth at six feet deep?

Vertiginous possibilities! Vertiginous possibilities!
shouted the other.

Old Ousep regretted
his sharp ear.
He wondered if pronouns was something that happened
to them as he himself, he knew, would become
a Kochi beach. He, he knew,
would turn to dust.

I don't mean to upset
you, said Ousep, but is something happening
to you that never happened before?
Or, were you always
a personal pronoun?

> Came the reply: I am rightfully reduced
> to a grammatical pronoun;
> in life and death I'm doomed, for death is
> a displaced name for a linguistic predicament
> and I am a personal

Pronoun, added Ousep,
hoping the other would remain
a friend. Not shout.

> Instead heard sighing low monotones of how long, long, long,
> how very long, he had been writing;
> writing while so young and all; writing
> into his old age too; what is there but writing,
> this play
> with words,
> language.
> Said the personal pronoun
> proffering another lesson
> (the same) in linguistics,

Cut short by Ousep's impatience in old curiosity: what did you
write about?

> I cannot decide, he said,
> the answer to your question,
> and not just that, but it is
> that I cannot decide whether
> your question is, after all, a question
> at all.

That's all right, said Ousep, but what did
you write about?

> You'll say I wrote about this or
> about that, but that is not
> what I meant at all;
> that is not it, at all.

Ousep now, very curious: so, what
did you write about?

> Yours, came the voice, so much like extermination! Yes, I
> wrote in *Le Soir*
> not just that once, but many times, and it wasn't I, said
> the personal pronoun.
> but it wasn't I…

The personal pronoun, offered Ousep. Yes! The "I"
of then, the "I" of now all just…

In chorus the two said: a personal pronoun.
I didn't mean it at all and that is not what I meant at all; that is
not it, at all.

What did you not mean at all? persisted Ousep,
his Kochi curiosity unrelenting.

That! said the pronoun, is a non-question!
You just don't ask such a personal

Pronoun, chimed in Ousep, now used to such abuse; yet asked again:
what did you write about?
And his left ear rang again.

    Challenge!!!!
    Undermine!!!!
    Destabilize!!!!
    Subvert!!!!
    Deconstruct!!!!!

Ousep listened to
gibberish
in English,
the sighing in low monotones — then
                                              silence

Eternity, Now!

The unreality of time.
– J.M.E. McTaggart

Months yawn past unending iron
Creaking open always

Twice
Daily

Two more winters and freedom
At last! Endless labor

Outside our prison cell
Perennial roses and my companion

Bending to tend

Truth and Error in a Kaleidoscope

Now I know how, have the know-how, to invert perspectives [Ich habe es jetzt in der Hand, ich habe die Hand dafür, Perspektiven umzustellen]: first reason why a "revaluation of all values" is perhaps possible at all for me alone.
– Friedrich Nietzsche

    Just take a look, place your eye
here, through the viewing aperture of this kaleidoscope at sights un-
winding into intricate tight braids: the arc of a covenant,
some starred
cosmos, gems and diamonds,
O rare twirls of sunlight,
snatching your breath
away – this, this kaleidoscope is
a wonder, leaving you silent
at such a rare gift
of perspectives of what there is
on that side – these truths
of your truth.

But I am out here. Here. Outside
your kaleidoscope. I am watching you, your joy
and your wonder. Yet, I am here and not inside
your machine or eyes.
I now defy what you call perspectival
Truths. Truths that fetch odd patterns,
still stranger moods in an old friend. You now tire, I see, of staring
long hours into a child's plaything…
onto which has crawled a tiny serpent
intent, I see, on unwinding
not far from where rests
your eye…

    Come and see what indeed there is to all
your claims of the objective

truth in these creations of color and design, in a knowing
eye unafraid to see
or comprehend
another point of view on what you call certain
truth turning now red,
now blue,
now orange
and gold, in greens and browns...

Intent on striking, aiming for the place where rests your eye,

      burning in such profound glory of what
you may call heavenly or other-
worldly, is caught and released into this space
of this kaleidoscope...

Intent on striking, aiming for your eye....

Consequentialism at War

We have heard that half a million children have died. I mean, that is more children than died in Hiroshima. And, you know, is the price worth it?
– 60 Minutes *correspondent, Lesley Stahl*

I think that is a very hard choice, but the price, we think, the price is worth it.
– *United States Secretary of State, Madeleine Albright*

Sergeant Walia held what he'd found
                           in the town of Baghdad,
A child, still alive, whose face had been lifted
off her head, if such a thing is ever possible.
He looked around, our Sergeant of course, and saw his folk
moving stealthily and surely, rifles
pointing at the enemy
of the future – anyone who dared
                           to turn the wrong corner.

But one native lady wouldn't go away
and seemed so unafraid of anyone for that matter
that the sergeant wondered how she had
                           arrived
at this spot so well surrounded
                           by his own.
He glanced sideways at this body never still,
within a tent of a hijab or some cloak,
walking with him, keeping up with his strides,
even when he sped with the load in his arms.

He couldn't get a word to this companion for the wind kept blowing
                           his language far away,
while the lady, on her part, kept raising her palms,
her very self, to someone residing too far away,
or so it seemed to Sergeant Walia who turned
his eye to the same brown sky and then again

set his gaze quite steady at the friendly tank
                    parked beside the high-rise hotel.

At last by the tank, he yelled for help and heard
at that moment on the World at Six:
that all was well with the world at six
even in the land where allied soldiers were, for they,
said the voice, were sweating hard
                    for our great world's greater good.
He turned away, and along with the lady
strode the hotel steps
unhindered through the army-
glass-door where Lord Whiskeyfarm stood
chatting with his boss. Sir, said he,
                    our Sergeant of course,
just thought I'd fetch you the lesser evil;
        then handed him
        live load and lady.

Figure Skating

Freedom is the will to be responsible to ourselves.
— Friedrich Nietzsche

So part of being one and the same person throughout this bodily life is being continuously liable to account for my actions, attitudes, and beliefs to others within my community.
— Alasdair MacIntyre

                               You,

You do not see my heart
      dance, its shudder nothing
compared to   the swinging of my arms or legs
you have long admired   and now even more since
you lost your

head,

got drunk and brought home this plight
                         now shared with me and further apportioned
                                   for one conceived in my womb
also without a limb; nor do you

see the gush

from my eyes now
perhaps glistening on my face
as I turn away

from your view lest you slip

                   again

Groundbreaking

Writing unfolds like a game [jeu] that invariably goes beyond its own rules and transgresses its limits. In writing, the point is not to manifest or exalt the act of writing, nor is it to pin a subject within language; it is rather a question of creating a space into which the writing subject constantly disappears.
— Michel Foucault

Roland, Michel, and Friedrich meet again
in the sands to talk of where they left off
the time they wore dirt like shoes on barren soles,
when Friedrich came up with the idea,
their idea, of cutting a hole in a favorite doll, of pulling
out the substance so tightly stuffed behind
the bloated tummy and (they later found)
the head
of the two-armed,
two-legged
dumb creature whom they
quickly agreed they would
call 'the author.'

It is Friedrich, again, always, who explains why there
should be an end to this other.
It is he who points to
the grave injustice caused
by the author who plainly forces each
one of them to act only in a certain
manner. The doll, indeed, has mastery
over how they are to play:
they've made the author into
a soldier standing guard to their native land and now
fight a bitter war because they
are unsure
of what to call this new place;
so, they turn the author

into their brother who
changes them too instantly
into father, mother, and milkman, and indeed
even after the three have
sworn the author will never
be their child.

Upon such insult, it is decided:
proposed by Friedrich, the milkman, seconded by
mother and moved by father; or really – simply
executed or done. And the author is
depleted and soon discarded
in the dry sands where
the four played once upon a time
with each other. And now

after so long, once again in the clay, Friedrich says,
he'd like to be the milkman,
just for the sake of good old times,
and turns the other two instantly
into father and mother who decide
it is time to put an end
to such authorial mastery –
the two rip a hole and begin to
pour the milkman's substance inside out.

Pining

Nature has placed mankind under the governance of two sovereign masters, pain and pleasure. It is for them alone to point out what we ought to do, as well as to determine what we shall do.
— Jeremy Bentham

Palpitating hearts working the water out
of tongues drenched later by our kisses,
lip to lip, tongue to tongue, oneness
                                      staked

in a moment's knotting: of eyes and dreams
and limbs. Ours were minds that said please, please, please,
and then yesss to unblinking attraction
pulling you and me into this

tight marriage. This marks
what we now call our lives. I wonder how
we of normal intellect can make
such a leap on so little
a thing as a heart or the dream-
tongue that rested so often
on what we then felt

in stomach and throat. I
now call this plain heartburn and treat
with Pepto-Bismol, something
that you have become so adept at serving
each time I complain.

But what you will just not understand:
this is not the life I want – one devoid
of writers, and my name remembered
in higher circles than your world of pines

spreading roots into my very being,
cracking my pathways and me
presenting for all the world to see
this unkempt front so shameful,

even to me who has known –
albeit in some distant past –
success of which you have not
                         a clue.

And so: it's time for you to accept the pain
of divorce...

                        God
                    forgive us!
               Let's not speak
         of success and divorce.
     Just accept our faithfulness
  to each other all these years; and now
as I again serve this antacid it is my way of loving
you day by day without the dream we've dreamt of but it is
me and you bonded in this verb – love – to which your writers will
never be privy, not even for your dream's greater good but for you, as
              you stay awake,
              you beside me
               until we are
               laid to rest.

Speaking with the Dead

It is the role of the scholar to speak to the dead and to make the dead speak: "Stay, speak, speak, I charge thee speak".
— Stephen Greenblatt

You desire to speak with the dead actors of history,
men in black and white who wrote in colored
ink. At this you stare in long silence, lend
an Englishman's ear in style
most Roman,
when Shakespearean
scenes vanished before moneyed eyes
long familiar with all lip movements.

Your lips form verses learnt by rote in an empire
vigilant of its young;
ever vigilant as the young turn old
critics, as the now almost dead
talk in a new historicism with the dead text of a subject.
This aesthetic world –
literature, and that force –
power, society, history
over-determined.
This is the history of dead men and their dying
desire for what they lack – talk
with friends, enemies, the neutral or the others all retraced and laid

before silent readers and scholars
silenced, forbidden to interpret – you
in green blatting old desires lurking amongst the dead –
text.

What You Said

On dit.
– Michel Foucault

The author is therefore the ideological figure by which one marks the manner in which we fear the proliferation of meaning.... "What difference does it make who is speaking?"
– Michel Foucault

These words of yours, every character,
and number, comma and colon,
let me examine or *analyze*.
It is the right term.
Let this little red-ant amidst big grains, sugar in a diabetic's urine,
lick the fact of your word.
It is made text and its truth is hard,
not neutral against these
eyes and mouth. I am not
an empiricist –
who can be, now we've buried those fear-ridden,
Hobbes-to-Hume for that matter? I do know there is nothing
beyond this text,
this epistemology. I will
be true to these
words of yours: every character,
and number, comma and colon.
Now let me examine, rather analyze –
this type,
font,
paper,
screen,
all this,
all this the performance of a text –
this discourse.

I am
but beginning to speak
for I was thinking of what
I already knew, but thought it best
to know your name.
Thank you for
your willingness to analyze me,
even to categorize and find
the source or to quote
you,
analyze the type and the font
of all that I
am and say…

It doesn't matter at all what *you* say for who are you or I? It is
that which is said – it is said, by this
theoretician of world renown.
No fool out in the cold! But
it is said.
And suffice it that we have just that: what it is that is said of
every
character and
number,
comma and
colon
for me
(and you)
to analyze this discourse, for what you say now
was not what you said the other day
nor will be tomorrow.
How then am I to find the font of you who change – not
unlike the level of glucose in my pal, the diabetic I know?

        I hope your friend feels better soon,
        improves.
        But my recent physical shows

I do not have diabetes.
I assure you.
What I say is not under
the influence of drugs,
levels of glucose, but by my own
will,
choice much shaped, I admit,
by what is around me or
what I've learnt and
contemplated upon to fit a life
picked out of options galore
available to me and to
you as to many.
I speak who I am.
So, go ahead – examine me
not as if you would
the urine of a diabetic, crystals
formulated by chemicals uncontrolled,
but even as you would
your pal, the diabetic,
the one you say with passion
                                              you know.

Dandelions for Bhabha

Plant and not wholly plant
And so writ by the divine hand,
You'll say, this mimic is
A plain threat.

Almost a weed, yet not quite,
The subject of difference is
Not exactly recognizable in
Its ambivalence, its slippage

Between being almost
The same, but not quite.
Is it a plant? You say yes
And no. A weed, then? Yes,

You say, no. You cannot
Make up your mind for you insist
This one has taken up the looks
Without discarding its hooks.

You are dazzled, you say, again
Complain of all that is
Suffocating this space between
Great mimicry and downright mockery.

Its crime is: not to speak.
Its crime is to be
(In) your uncertainty
Of being.

migrants

A child away from home so long
Will not five years survive.
A bird so small, so frail and lone
Will soar without a sore.
When heads of parents shove it strong
From cliff, a tree, a door
The one falls right, the other wrong
As stranger turns a guide.

The bird it sings, it flies, and eats
Or so we understand.
But she, we see, is torn to bits
By crimes unheard at home.
A bundle of joy in feathers and crests
A bundle of nerves the other.
A singer bird and mad temptress
At last on snow shall meet.

Spivak

"Can the Subaltern Speak?"
— *Gayatri Spivak*

Good-lookin' lady sheathed in a saree,
And underneath? I suspect sneakers; hair
Trimmed like a widow's.

I know you've risen out of *Water*,
Refusing to drown or deny yourself
jouissance.

The year my mother dies in Toronto,
One thousand gather at King's Circle convinced
You are royalty;

With them I too, for a vision —
You. You whom I have
Studied, explained, and reinterpreted.

Your argued lecture goes well
(Your pages of footnotes Harvard respects);
You narrate; we settle into our chairs,

Glad to see you, hear you, know
You are speaking to us about yours
In so many words, ending only at

The question period.

One black woman, a student, I swear,
Shoots out of her chair to ask
One simple question.

"Who," she asks, "is your
Audience?" And I watch in horror as you
Crumble right before our eyes

In defense of a name
You cannot wring out of your chest;
One well hidden under so much pain.

One for so long adored and hated, criticized,
Crushed in bear-hugs, arrivals, departures…
Drawn-out goodbyes,

Frantic phone calls,
Refusals to speak,
Bad words

In an inherited tongue.
The unspeakable name even this woman
Cannot wrench out of you:

"Mother" or "my mother."
The moment you are caught
You just cannot speak.
In terror's stillness.

The subaltern weeps.

Jerome is One

the wonder
in his eyes the mystery
of creating a one year old
ugly in cake

the tremor
of the delivery room
the cutting
of the cord carried
through the year

a hand supporting
the back touching
finger on little finger

the disbelief believing wondering
joy

Jus' Thinkin'

The Storekeeper
— *Gavin Hood*

There is this short film I watch
On DVD where there is not a voice but
Things move,
A car rolls,
The door closes, and then a single

Shot.

All the people are Black
There, in Africa:
The shopkeeper,
The thief, and
The little children who will soon come after
Candies. Then the director, chatty,
Talks over the silence. And I
Think: blast the damn bastard!
Relax into buttered popcorn well after
The tool cuts into wood,
Into iron, and into the frontiers of
My peace.

I finally write his fate into the palm of my hand
That time he kills the night watchman.

I think the victim of repeated burglary
Is one smart chap as he lays a trap
Of plain white twine, zig-
Zagging low across the doorway and through
The sturdy black trigger. I anticipate
The stealthy entrance,
The trip,

The tug,
The final boom.

But no one is prepared for
Someone's darling

Three-year-old raising her little head,
Dragging her bleeding
Body into the vista of my
thought.

Theorizing Difference

Watch the letter P stand up
trim but for its seat of thought, then
look at the letter B, and you just cannot help but
smile at how quickly the big brain and the pot belly
together made an earlier companion of
your tender learning days. Yet, as Saussure says,
if a PIN is a pin it is so because it is neither
a pun nor a bin or, in short, it gains
a reputation by being just different.
But is that which a bachelor sticks into his shirt
upon losing his first button and then simply learns to
stud himself with a weird habit? Or is it
what is so well known as something
you have to have to identify yourself, or
another as not you? Is it not what
you add to the end of someone's mail? How about
a rolling pin? Perhaps you don't care
a pin what a pin is! Such Empsonian
excitements proliferate in
the very best ambiguities – wait! perhaps it is
after all what a North American woman might stick
right into her sturdy head before
she is, as they say, pinned
down by someone she cannot tell on?

Singing of Difference

It is with difference that we know each other; that
I am not you and you
not another. We later use difference to mark off
not just I versus you, but us versus them;
what happened, we wonder, to the first difference that
made of you and me
this us?

(Oh! Let us just say it is time to join in a chorus led by Derrida:
'the absence of transcendental signified extends the domain and
the play of signification infinitely.')
And so let us sing: anything goes,
anything goes
where there is
no deity.

And so let us sing: anything goes,
anything goes
where there is
no deity.

Five-year-old Celia scrubbed her little chest from black
to blue or the color purple. Since every way she turned
her arms appeared, she covered them with linen
spun from shame. One noon she squeaked up to her bully:
my soul at least is white. Thirty years thence
he reminded her this when whiteness oozed from
her bruised private part. Her tone, then, was a B flat:
there is unity in all this diversity.

And so let us sing: anything goes,
anything goes
where there is
no deity.

Oliver Twist turns the wrong corner;
he asks for more to still his gnawing
hunger. The shopkeeper? He flings hot water,
boiling water at his third-world figure.
The boy? He refuses to die or deny.
He invokes a humanitarian
crowd that beats up the keeper,
sends him back into his own water.

And so let us sing: anything goes,
anything goes
where there is
no deity.

The edible man is bursting at his seams
without even eating his desired fill.
At the back of the bus he hides his birth.
Then walks up to him a gentleman
who clearly says: fatso. And yet again,
fatso. Each ef-word enunciated, the sibilant rings
the bus to a full stop. The edible man,
he turns turnip, he descends before
his destination. He cries with no one,
to no one in particular:
what's the difference?

And so let us sing: anything goes,
anything goes
where there is
no deity.

And thus, and thus, in endless regress difference is
turned into the odd-sounding *differance* whose
effect of difference is deferred and you begin to
tolerate this eternal difference to the point of saying:
'The mind is its own place, and in itself

Can make a heaven of hell, a hell of heaven,'
only thinking you are quoting a great English poet
and not in the least bit Satan himself.

And so let us sing: anything goes,
anything goes
where there is
no....

from the Canadian pew

A step at a time as the Church bells chime
A five-year-old lady moves beautifully.
Her head held high, she walks down the aisle,
And follows her people to the seat of the faithful.
She kneels most gravely and stays thus bravely
For the first two minutes and then slightly fidgets.
She tosses her topknot and that is a start
For soon she rises and glitters in surprises.
She bends suddenly for a book well hidden
And then she straightens to see what happens.
She talks to her mother and then to her father
And nods when told not to be bad.
She prays the Our Father, then her eyes wander.
Her head turns around to the ones behind:
She eyes suspiciously and then curiously
The young brown couple who pray with trouble.
She fans her hot face and leans in a daze,
Awakens in a start accomplishing a ____.
Now on her way out she tells in one shout,
'At least I did it in the pew.'

Prophet-Prostitute

Dark damsel, lovely woman,
Prophet, prostitute, all in one;
Bearer of seven demons, demon,
Deer-eyed temptress, sinner stoned?

Medicine woman, great embalmer,
Of resurrection lonely seer,
To frightened folks then a speaker,
The church's rock, and its honor?

Rock, shelter, La Madeleine,
House of refuge of ex-whores,
Apostle to Apostles, Magdalene,
Riddle of churches, pain of patriarchs.

Translation

A good translation is a creative reconstruction in one language of ideas originally expressed in another and it must, of course, strive to make the original intelligible in terms that will make sense to its readers... it may be asked, do not contemporary international languages such as English have the resources necessary for making intelligible other traditions?
– Brian Barry

The new thing in Early Modern is to read
Works of the Arab in Translation.
The Arab, after all, cannot speak
A single word in English, plain or just about
When he does – your Texas toast is skimpy –
His accent mighty thicker. Ha! Ha! Excuse me!
Seriously! You cannot write a paper in Early Modern
Unless you read the Arab in translation.
It is important, you see, to know the other side –
With or without butter – what can you do?
You take what you get in translation,
You've tried, and if the Arab doesn't write
In English plain and simple read him
In translation, the Arab translated; tran-slated,
If he doesn't get it, what can you do?
He should take all he can get when we read
Him in translation.
It's commonsense, to read him in translation
Creatively, interpreted; we cannot mistranslate.
After all, an orange used to be a norange –
No marmalade? –
And a farmer husbonda; if you can translate
His color to olive on the night of nine eleven
That's clearly translated for it isn't white
Man's land where there are, after all, no olives
To translate you to the truth of history slated
For translation: all truth can, after all, be translated
After the Death of the Author or his Mother.

Our cosmopolitan tongue, rich, international,
Can even better comprehend the poverty,
The skimpy sketches in other languages,
Languages with little grammar, no structure.
Ours abounds in vocabulary, from arsenic to zero
It is all Arabic. Ha! Ha! Ha! Ha! Seriously!
Our language will now, in eternity, create,
Translate, profitably assimilate, God or Mammon,
Vice versa. *Pardon* my Latin! O… my French!
Briefly.
The new.
Thing.
In Early Modern.
Is.
To read.
Works of.
The Arab in translation.

To Talisman

History

If modernism had tried to anchor in consciousness a centre which could no longer hold—the conscience of the heroic, socially alienated artist—postmodernism had shown us an even darker side of modernity and the aporias of the aesthetic. It had shown that there is nothing for consciousness to be anchored to: no universal ground of truth, justice, or reason, so that consciousness itself is thus "decentred," no longer origin, author, location of intentional agency but a function through which impersonal forces pass and intersect – Dover Beach displaced by an international airport lounge.
– Patricia Waugh

How do I reveal the grain of hope buried under
skeletons of great-grandparents, grand-aunts, and uncles
aged four to forty-nine, friends of family, children,
robbed with corporate efficiency of all but official identities –
beggar, criminal, vagrant, Negro, Jew, Gypsy –
who left behind those with so little memory;
how do I show alive the speck of truth so well hidden
of what happened to once-upon-a-time's beloved?

Stories told, retold, are half heard in this efficiency-
driven world; today's flickering, fast-changing, remote-
controlled virtual reality is someone's making,
with power, with knowledge, of hate.

Name him Luther or Himmler or say
it wasn't the myth but an entire system,
center-less, that constructed and deconstructed
a million times to deliver with the precision of math
injustice to just some people too lowly,

while the too highly strut impressively to
delegate the vulgar task of dispensing:
shave her, cut his right ear off, work her to death.
And this is the literal truth, until

a sign rises in the East and
you stand knowing
there is nothing
signified;

until you are
replaced by interpretation that knows
neither right nor wrong;

until you are
called by the nick-
name of ideology;

and Universal Justice is dragged
to Auschwitz.

The Prophet's Cup

The year is today and I have opened my mouth to utter
Full-scale damnation or simply state the plain fact—
This city will have no water.

And now that I have said as much I am doomed to tread
The oil sands where children of ravens shall wait upon me
With toast and tea. And I shall plan my last sleep

Under the broom tree. But. Grandchildren of angels
Wake me up with naan out of a hot tandoor
And lead me to a secret brook that is fast dying
Before I begin the tour: around the world
In forty days and forty nights.

the walls are ridden with holes
the roof is still on
she must have taken the children and joined
the thousands on the roads
the artillery pounding
all night
long

You have ordered the great slaughter of
Those born and unborn.
Everywhere is a silent cry. Even so.

a crater appears, vaporizing
a mother and her child
it is time now
help at the stretcher parties
sew up
the broken head
keep heading to the sea
it is drinking
it is death-dealing

So I had slept.

the weary foot lifts
over the dead and
the dying

Between the prophecy and the prayer,
Between the king and the queen,
Between the rain and the desert sand
My cloaked face awaits –
Well after the rock-splitting quake,
The typhoon, and the blaze –
A gentle whisper and
A sip of peace.

Only Hands

two hands the color of color
spread before a word
from mouths of mounties
government's best pals
whose second tongue speaks

the hands taut, the nails trimmed
hide well the first word, the second tongue
as mounties mount their moral mountain
glide governors elegantly across
the himalayan rockies
the rocking himalayas

two palms really, turned the other way
nothing more; just two hands
spread before the post, the herald, the star
carving humans into diviners
readers with all the right moves
cowering before the doom displayed
reading the frontpage terrorist

The Person in my Eye

If I say, "It will not be me, but one of my future selves," I do not imply that I will be that future self. He is one of my later selves, and I am one of his earlier selves. There is no underlying person who we both are.
— Derek Parfit

Looking into my eye you catch yourself
Nice and whole, top to toe — your
Self, you will say,
But it is my eye.

    I am right now staring into this
Nostril, the left one, the one
With less vibrissae than the other,
Which I examined in our last conversation and wish
Not to look into again.

It is not normal in this culture
To look up people's noses.
To look into my eyes and see
Yourself in me is nothing
More than some Camera
Obscura with power
To shred you with light
Or end you with my lid.

    My culture forbids such staring
Eye to eye, but I did try to and have reached
As far as this nose but cannot rise any further
                               than that ear.

Please look into my eye as a normal being should —
Even a dog looks another in the eye.
Look into my eye and see the myth that is
You, so whole and unified you claim, is
Nothing more than what determines

You at this moment
In my eye.

    I have been concentrating for so long
Upon each higher-up anatomy
That I do not know if our cultures together have
Broken the body…

You have a point there, which is
My point that to culture belongs
The so-called self and there is no one
Outside culture, no…

    Yes, destroyed what we call core
Identity
In such discontinuity
Of anatomy…

Wait, do not rush off even if that is your culture,
But stay to finish off this conversation that you
And I have begun.

    This nose, that ear, or some eyes just cannot
Expect such obedience
In me…

But wait! It is me telling you to stay with
Me!

Are You a Feminist?

Then strain out the water before you boil your tea today
Of children flung
Bluck
Bluck
Bluck
One-two-three,
The oldest first and the youngest
Last, into the well-water – Oh so natural, water.

Don't ask why you must strain it out if you are, after all,
Boiling. At least don't ask today when
She lies wet and moaning – a bitch in her
Last throes, skeletal arms pawing
The imaginary liquid,
Reaching out in several directions –
When she alone is lifted dripping, grabbing
Fistfuls of leaden air
Fit to be bottled, sealed, and sold for a buck or two or
Three.

Ask later, after she has been zapped, then prodded by the police;
After she has confessed to not being
A good mother,
A good wife
(She was a good daughter;
This she insists even after
An hour's interrogation),
After she has confessed to
Quarrelling or arrogance, to
Earning or greed
(After all, they have seen her purse:
They found her day's wages tightly tied
In a piece of deep blue cloth
In her shopping basket

Upturned in the middle of her swept hut),
And after she has matched all the synonyms
Logically, and is made to look twice
Her own middle age, and marched off
To be fed, at last, with murderers.

You won't ask why you must strain it out
For you are, after all, boiling.

The Taj Mahal

I looked at the Taj with my mind's eye
And saw: immortality of marble, sheen of stones,
Wonderous waters, majestic domes,
A love eternal. I saw you Shah,
Your love of pulchritude flowing from Noor.
Her curves you carved into the Mahal;
In the rivulets you caught her tears.
But why did she shed tears before one like you?
Possibly during umpteen labours.
Was it her largeness that made the Taj so big?

Big and beautiful.
I will not see the celebration of a dead woman.

To Talisman

A few people in the country become wealthier; GDP statistics, for what they are worth, look better, but ways of life and basic values are threatened... This is not how it has to be.
— Nobel Laureate, Joseph Stiglitz

I will give you a talisman. Whenever you are in doubt, or when the self becomes too much with you, apply the following test. Recall the face of the poorest and the weakest man whom you may have seen, and ask yourself, if the step you contemplate is going to be of any use to him. Will he gain anything by it? Will it restore him to a control over his own life and destiny? In other words, will it lead to swaraj [freedom] for the hungry and spiritually starving millions? Then you will find your doubts and your self melt away.
— Mahatma Gandhi

Very bad! Very bad! she said, shaking her head.
Now this way swung one earring, now the other way.
You have, she said, showing off her rotten teeth, bad-luck
sitting on your chest, and touched ever so lightly

my breast, telling me
my pendant, green and heart-shaped, was not the cause
but something else, hidden:

deep inside me palpitation,
giddiness at visions of gold, heaped coins secured
under the blanket bargained from the Tibetan woman with the
babe on her back –
she made as if toward me, froze, yet her earrings stirred to a breeze;

deep inside me the incessant caressing
shapes, textures, coolness of a new Bugatti weaving milky
highways to highland resorts, paradises...
bulging biceps closing in on bikinis threadbare,
threadbare, threadbare....
She caught my eye, but slipped my view to the ripple by her ear;

deep inside me I wake up exhausted
having wrestled my demons all night,
steady my sight, unwavering poise at the top

of Mount Everest, where sometimes I chance upon ones
called the natives –

trembling men with wiry wives and children shriveling....
At that moment, she extended to me a Turkish amulet, like turquoise,
said: Wear it! Wear it! Always! And swayed her head like an elephant.

Excited children shrivel in the stark gaze
of the pitiless sun displaying not the cost
of their lives but the side-roads of my itinerary.

I stared in shock at my talisman
on which was engraved
a faceless child who should bring me
good luck.

Teach me to never forget
The place of my visit, where the bodies I rode on
Still lie supine.

Milk for Ganesha?

Little Ganesha opened his eyes
To see the passing crowd.
But even with his eyes shut tight
He knew it passed him by.
He waited sprawled. He listened.
That sound, that thud stop thud.
He waited thus for hours or days
Or years maybe, who knows?
A fly checked now a leaky eye
And crawled below to nostril.
He swayed his head to dislodge it
And slept at this effort.
Now, in his sleep he heard a thud,
A stop, and then a thud.
He smiled and opened his mouth and swallowed.
His throat hurt.
It woke him up and made him listen
To all the other thuds.
He heard then strong and clear,
"Milk for Ganeshji"
And smiled. He heard even in sleep
This lullaby, this chant.
Again he awoke to the unmistakable thud,
Then stop, and then thud.
Ganesha twitched his lips in smile.
The sound, it passed him by.

Compassionate Choice

To please no one will I prescribe a deadly drug nor give advice which may cause his death.
– Hippocrates

To die proudly when it is no longer possible to live proudly. Death of one's own free choice, death at the proper time, with a clear head and with joyfulness, consummated in the midst of children and witnesses: so that an actual leave-taking is possible while he who is leaving is still there.
– Friedrich Nietzsche

Naked on the verandah and bowing
to the rhythm of visions, he stands
knocking, knocking, his head against
the talking wall while the hen remains
beside her chicks, alert to the eagle's circle.
No one is thinking here; none can
think clearly enough to say – I am:
these are dumb beasts of burden to
the nation.

The screaming begins at the wall
when one chick is taken.
Such pain no one can endure to
see or live, no, no; a human is
howling for relief that lies in the
hand of another – preserved
in the files of superior civilization.
Surely some action is at hand; surely
Action T4² is at hand. The eagle
shall return another day, to lift
a weakling chick which has not
strength to run to its mother's wing.
But today? Today my brother is being
readied for the mercy kill.

---
² Euthanasia in Nazi Germany.

La La Liberté

Your cap is at a smart angle,

                                              your flag
the right white, black and red
of blood,
      your breasts are properly
bare,

you're okay to insist on riding upon

dead men's chests,

drenched women,

cowering families, another Delacroix

right,   at the crossroad of what's

what's wrong.
        But if
you really must then
go ahead, cut

across

                                    the zebra, declare you
                                    cannot

comprehend the white-
on-red ARRÊT,
          say the French have
          their own culture,
     you yours,

                                  that you jus' ain't gonna

(what's the right word?)
you just ain't gonna—
capitulate,
    when in your own

car; if you must, then go ahead,

        my million dollar
        baby, please go right ahead and exercise

your freedom at
            the traffic lights.

Soodo Klaasik

As whales wear glaziers, rabbits
snow gear;
As the drawn foot
in a hidden pit at rear is
trapped; like each scream
is to hear, each locked woman finds
limb and lip to
proclaim her fear;
every human does one thing and is
near: in existing within
at least lives;
Themselves – as selves;
yourselves in word and act,
screaming
What I do I am: for that I'm here.

I say no more: the wise one
wises;
begs for prudence: that makes
virtuous all performances; performs what
one entirely is – after death. For Time enters
all sounds and spaces,
steady in rhythm,
and prompt in presence to
itself in the features of
our own faces.

Friends of Thomas More

The breeze visits upon gray waves
A curl in solitude,
Another head.
Mannequins forty years too old
Displayed at the roadside salon.

They certainly knew how close they were
Each time they refused to bend
At the knee, resisted the ancestral itch
To bow, bare the nape before the State
That changed with every wind.

Ten months too late the westerly once again makes its rounds,
The heads chopped off from dangling frames
Secret lessons for those still bending,

And bloodily arranges exhibits upon the London Bridge
Tossed at last to an eternal
Splash.

Professional Secrets I

Professional profs these, they hoard up for firing times.
Slash, they say, slash. Not a hundred, they say,
Just fifty give back to the university; you give back
How about eighty back to the university; fifty knows
Nothing of eighty nor eighty of fifty. Confidentiality.

We love them these stewards who know to slash
When, where, why, and how. These make the university
Proud, and our homes brace to embrace such a guest
Into our porch, our arms. Our brain –
It is sizzling
New numbers much lighter;

It is heavy in complicity.

To . . .

run
your hose
and wear
a mini;
to whisper
on phone
(the manager passes by);
to forget
your spoon
and eat
your rice
at work;
to come and be
told –
have canadianexperience
first;
to be born
a woman
coloured;
to be
inconvenient.

Professional Secrets II

They walk with secrets, these professors,
down corridors, up classrooms, in driveways
smiling sometimes, or just serious as silence,
hoarding their secrets like rats in better times.

They walk briskly
past you or
stay bent down

under the weight of books, you think,
when the secrets weigh
on lives – like
the cancer hidden
in a coughing chest, like conscience
lost in rhetoric.

To kiss a little book

I feel… that it is impossible for us, with our limited means, to attempt to educate the body of the people. We must at present do our best to form a class who may be interpreters between us and the millions whom we govern; a class of persons, Indian in blood and colour, but English in taste, in opinions, in morals, and in intellect.
– Thomas Babington Macaulay

Afraid to breathe I tip-toe, a child
'midst lonely aisles in search of dusty friends,
now peeking when fat fathers stand busy
as I check name, to bosom hold, then smell

and kiss the little book gently laid
against left hand, most grateful for
promised hours of deep friendship. How rare
that only we knew, none else, the fluttering

wonder, curious joy, the greed of speech-
less words on paper, vibrant worlds
in hours gifted away from adults' hate-
days or years, their brooding fault-finding.

A golden book with a Norman princess,
remember? Who wore a long
braid and loved Prince Whoever first or last?
That too forget, but not the hate unleashed

as races, families, clans devoured
other people's lands, and life itself
and me, who prayed that they marry soon
before the queen arrived to destroy such love

in little books with faded covers
unseen by all except a child in search
of alphabets, words, the tale's solace:
a reader colored into a postcolonial world.

Santa!

Dance bells and church bells, cycle bells and door bells
Fire bells, ice-cream bells, phone bells and maid bells.
Jingle jingle bells and all such fun.
A tiny little girl now laughs, she skips
To jingle jingle jingle in the school compound.
Ice-cream and chocolates, jujubes and gifts
Sports and games. Dances and songs.
Jingle jingle jingle she trots in step.
Horses now pass and someone in a car.
She learns how to sing that jingle jingle bells.
Running in a race and lining up for more.
Lining up again, (no, not for penicillin).
She rushes to the fore, then stops in her tracks.
She stares at this monster, now in its worst.
Bearded and red, this thing is so big.
She screams half way when dragged into lap.
She clenches her fist and presses her eyes.
This man, this monster, this stranger from the west.
Her darling soon enough and might as well be.

War and Peace 101: Final Exam

The way in which the other presents himself, exceeding the idea of the other in me, we here name face.
– Immanuel Levinas

Though her name means 'the sun' in English, 18-month-old Shams may never be able to experience sunlight in her life again. Half her face was blown away in an explosion in Baghdad, leaving her eyes buried under badly burnt skin.
– IRIN, Humanitarian News and Analysis, UN Office for the Coordination of Humanitarian Affairs

What do you do when you encounter
The unspeakable horror of the faceless
Face – a child, with everything
But a face, squirming in hell's agony
And not a sound from
Her mouth plundered
In an invasion of
A life;
When you just cannot
Know her pain
Or that of her mother whose language
You do not speak? Can you look

Into the faceless face and not recognize
The capital crime of your silence,
Of the injustice that you authorized when
You turned your face a certain way or simply
Away; not suspect that
                       there are a thousand more

Whose faces have been mined, made devoid
Of identity after your people
Categorized the children carefully
                       into a group?

How do you interpret this performance,
This phenomenon of a loss-of-face
Or the scarring of self-image
Or the threat of annihilation to
Personhood;
This inability to imagine the one
Whom you now will into your person
To love in empathy?

What do you do when you
Encounter the unimaginable
Horror, the faceless face,
The other?

Made in the USA
Lexington, KY
07 June 2018